Life-long Effects of Child Sexual Trauma - In Drawings

Life-long Effects of Child Sexual Trauma – In Drawings

VIOLA B. MECKE PH.D., ABPP

A Prologue to the Story

*I*would like to have this story about a child who was sexually traumatized about the age of four and one-half years to become known. I want to show how the effect of a single episode may skew a person's development and life forever after. Anne was a precocious child, reading and writing before the age of five. Her development was drastically affected by a single unexpected episode, an episode that overwhelmed her feelings, interfered with her thinking and learning, and marred her personality development.

Her experience is not an unusual one. Too many children have experienced some type of sexual stimulation before the age of eighteen. Thirty-four percent of *reported* cases of sexual abuse were perpetrated on children younger than nine years of age. Further, research conducted by Centers for Disease Control estimates that approximately one in four girls are and one in six boys are sexually abused before the age of 18.[i] And, it is further estimated that only thirty per cent of incidences are reported, due to shame, fear of publicity, or guilt of the abused child and families. Another study suggests that 85 per cent[ii] of children do not tell anyone about the abusive incident.

In my experience in working with children over a period of many years, I often enough treated sexually traumatized children and/or reported to the judicial system about the traumatic episodes. I use the term *traumatized* because not all cases involve penetration. Sexual abuse includes any person who willfully and lewdly commits any lewd or lascivious act, upon or with the body, of a child under the age of 14 years with the intent of arousing, appealing to, or gratifying lust, passions or sexual desires of that person or the child, is guilty of a felony.[iii]

The focus of this paper is the effects of child sexual abuse – an abuse that destroys the child's faith in people and in the environment. It destroys a sense of safety, of trust, of security – no longer feeling protected by adults. Let me describe some experiences that sexually traumatized children have to deal with.

A boy, four or five years old, came into the office. He had been dismissed from kindergarten because of touching other boys' penises. While playing in my office, he constantly was touching his penis or rubbing it against the furniture. What had happened? Mother had masturbated him to help him sleep – for most of his life Or a seven- year- old girl who had spent a weekend with her father, by court order. She returned to her mother, clinging to her fiercely. She wanted to know if she had to spend time with her father. What had happened? The father had taken the daughter for a "fun" weekend. They slept in a motel. The father had her sleep in her underwear. He also slept in his underwear – in the same bed. But pulling her close to him in the bed, the girl reported, "He got real big!" And he was rubbing me in my privates. There was no actual intercourse. This is sexual trauma. Legally, it is a "lewd or lascivious act" upon a minor.

One more example. An adult reported that during her early teens, probably beginning about the age of twelve, her stepfather would put her to bed, touching and massaging her sexually. After her menstrual periods began, he would stimulate her sexually with his fingers; then one night, he penetrated her. She only remembers passing out. After that he would routinely have sex with her. The repercussions for the girl resulted in early promiscuity, but without climax. When she married, the complaints of her husband was that she could not respond sexually no matter what he tried! She was robbed of a lifetime of physical and emotional pleasure.

The attitudes of some adults are confusing, and un-insightful, for they are blind to the damage of over-stimulating a child emotionally. There is a widespread belief that the child does not remember, that he/she will forget, that he/she will "get over it." Prior to maturation, the emotional system is not prepared for the tremendous over-activation of the sexual system; it is like an explosion to the neurological system.

In one incident, I was asked to report to the court about the harm done to a five-year-old girl who had been sexually molested by an adult male, her uncle. Her uncle had obtained an attorney and a psychologist. In talking with the other attorney, he reported that he was prepared to defend the uncle. The consulting psychologist firmly believed no harm could have been done to the child. To the contrary, it was normal and good for the child to be prepared for adult sexuality. That was unbelievable! Yet, here was a colleague with little empathy or knowledge or understanding or awareness of the damage of the physical act, let alone of the enduring psychological and emotional repercussions which would endure throughout the child's life.

Literature and research on the effects of trauma in childhood abound, but seldom have the long-term effects of sexual, or other traumata, been traced throughout the life of a person. The drawings presented here suggest that to a certain extent, children may recover from sexual trauma and resume an apparently normal life. However, the scars linger throughout the lifetime and affect their personalities and their everyday behaviors.

I have loved my clinical work with children and families. There was no greater pleasure than helping parents meld together with their children into a happy family. To see the tenderness for the children renewed, the partnership of husband and wife consolidated, and the family unit smiling to be together, brought both joy and glad tears to my heart. There have been many times when problems faced by the family meant that scars of unfortunate events were to be accepted before harmony and love were re-established within the family. Such are the enduring scars of child abuse, whether they are physical, emotional or sexual.

To return to my story. This child, Anne, was brought to therapy because the parents were concerned about her behavioral changes. She had changed from a quiet and docile child to a silent, withdrawn, sometimes stubborn person.

All names and places have been changed to protect the identity of all.

It is my aim to show how this child told the story of her sexual trauma, of her progress toward recovery, and the life-long effects of the incidence — as told by the drawings she made, before and after the event.

Acknowledgments

I am so grateful for suggestions and reading provided by Diana Greenwood. Her help in editing the work was invaluable and the enlightening conversations were a delight.

For the valuable support and encouragement of my brother, William Bloom.

For the interest and support of all those persons, male and female, who suffered child sexual trauma and were eager to have this information public. They wanted to share that the effects have affected their life in many ways, often unknown. And, in part, gave them a knowledge of relationships with people that served to guide many of their choices.

Table of Contents

One

WHAT IS A TRAUMA

As I started to write about the effects of a "trauma" on a child, it seemed requisite to present a clear picture of "trauma". The word "trauma" has become an increasingly popularized word, leaving an unclear picture of what it is and of its impact on a person. Originally trauma referred to a physical wound; it is now used to represent a wound to the personality as well. The power of a single traumatic event may change behavior, thought processes, emotional functioning and even neurological processes.

A traumatic experience is like an earthquake that shakes the individual's innermost being. It tears apart the personality. As in an earthquake, tremors may follow. At the worst, a tremor involves a reliving of the traumatic event at an inopportune time, intruding unexpectedly into life. This return of the trauma may be triggered by some similar, present stimuli that is reminiscent of the traumatic event. Other tremors may come such as in sleeplessness, nightmares, unexpected aggression, stormy outbursts, cringing with fears, withdrawal into aloneness, for example. Trauma leaves bruises that may be slow to heal; the scars may be easily reopened; and, it never really disappears. Healing may come, but deep within the person is a hole the earthquake leaves – its power remains to affect the person even much later in life. The "run-off" affects the psyche and behavior. For example, Anne, in our story, suffered a trauma between the ages of four and five; ever after, she had a crisis every four or five years in life, upsetting her personal and/or professional relationships.

As an earthquake also alters the structure and appearance of the earth, so may a trauma affect the core of the person. Studies on the neurological effects of trauma have consistently shown structural and functional neurological changes. In general, the more protracted and intense the trauma, the more serious the damaging effects on the brain. An important consideration: the damage that the brain has suffered may, to some extent, be modified with good therapeutic measures.[iv]

Let me go to the roots of psychological thinking. Freud recognized the impact that a trauma has on a person. He wrote, trauma "shatters the foundations of his life" and continues: "in a very short space of time (trauma) subjects the mind to such a very high increase of stimulation that assimilation or elaboration of it can no longer be effective by normal methods..." [v]

To shatter the foundation of life, is to affect the way the person *thinks* about life and the environment – no longer is life safe; he/she becomes ever aware that danger may lurk. Trauma affects the way the person *behaves*. The person may avoid similar situations, may become more aggressive, obstinate, cringing, shyness, etc. And, trauma affects the *emotional life* of the person; for example, there is more fear, sensitiveness, sadness, withdrawal, etc.

All too often, adults dismiss the effects of trauma on a child. "He will get over it" "She will soon forget it." "They are so young, it will not affect them." The effects are actually more deleterious with children, for the experience becomes an integral part of the personality. It becomes a foundation for their understanding of life. To the contrary, children are more vulnerable: they have fewer experiences that might help them to understand; they have fewer resources of responding to protect themselves; and they are physically smaller and less powerful. A child does not forget.

I will try to show within this essay that a traumatic episode affects the deepest part of the personality. As we look at the drawings of this one child, we can see the symbolic follow-through of the sexual abuse and learn how it has affected her behavior and personality.

Two

THE STORY OF ANNE

In Drawings

Our story begins when Anne is three years old. Around four years, ten months old she was sexually abused. Her drawings will date and show that she suffered a sexual trauma and depict her slow recovery from the event. I present eleven pictures that she drew without being requested or interpreted from over two hundred that her parents saved, along with two pictures Anne drew at the age of 45 at my request. But first let me provide some background about Anne.

Anne was the second child born to her parents. She had a sister, Vicky, ten years older and a sister, Marie, two years younger. She came from a stable, middle-class family whose members were closely bonded to each other. Vicky was her mother's helper and often took care of her younger sisters. In turn, Anne played caregiver to Marie, telling her what to do, and even taking her to the bathroom in the middle of the night. They lived in a small suburban town, in close relationships with their neighbors. Her father was an engineer who travelled often for his job. Her mother, a nurse by training, was mainly a stay-at-home mom, who took care of the family needs.

Anne had many aunts, uncles and cousins. Sometimes in the summer, the family would visit relatives in a distant State. This was exciting for her and her sisters, for they loved the visits. It was a time for freedom, love and family games. It was here that our story has its start.

Her parents described Anne as a child with curiosity about everything from an early age. For instance, she was curious about the contents of cupboards and, as a three-year-old, would take everything out of the lower cupboard, just to see and name what was there. Even at three years of age, Anne had to replace everything. Another example of her curiosity: When her father repaired the car, Anne would sit on the fender and watch him – asking question after question – "What are you doing, Daddy?" She had an early interest in words and was reading and writing by four years old. She also spent hours drawing pictures. Anne's home life was permissive but with guidance and responsibilities.

The Drawings

Children speak through their drawings and art work. Their spontaneous drawings, especially, reveal the child's view of the world, some statement about him or herself, and/or feelings about the family and of the social environment.

Two scoring procedures were necessary to study Anne's pictures thoroughly. My first aim was to know something about Anne's developmental level. Clinical psychologists have developed standard procedures to evaluate the drawings of a person to provide a view of the developmental level and intellectual capabilities of the child. This research had its beginning with the work of Florence Goodenough in 1926. Since then, procedures have improved and become useful providing some insight into the personality development and emotional difficulties, as well. The procedures developed by Nagliere (1988)[vi] were used for scoring Anne's developmental and intellectual level. Generally speaking, the ratings are based on the completeness of the figures drawing and the style of drawing. The scores are given for picture as AE. AE represented the age level at which the average child would draw a similar picture.

The second scoring system provided a qualitative analysis of the drawing, using the system devised by McCarthy (1990).[vii] This system is used to identify emotional problems and more specifically, sexual trauma in children. The signs of sexual trauma may be evidenced through specific distortions of facial and bodily features. Summarizing, these signs include: an emphasis on the nose through a penile-suggestive elongation with or without an inner dot or a "pig-like" nose; elongated distortions of the ear; distortions of the mouth as a circular-open mouth or an arc-formed mouth with circular additions to the edges; unusual body features such as lack of the lower body, emphasis on the genital area, unusual attention to the feet and/or displacement of bodily parts. The qualitative discussion for Anne's drawings follow the scoring of each picture.

With each of her drawings, I will show her actual or chronologic age (CA) and developmental age (AE).

Picture l: CA = 3-0 years; AE – 4.3 years

The Drawings

Picture 1. (CA = 3.0 years; AE = 4.3 years). It is a picture of a baby girl with eyes, nose, mouth, hair, a body with arms and legs, and a belly button. Anne's picture includes details that are not expected until a child is 4 years 3 months old. This indicates that Anne is an intelligent, even precocious, child. Scales developed by psychologists show agreement between drawing ability and intellectual abilities.[viii] The drawing also shows that Anne is a sensitive child with her eyes open to the world evidenced by the arms extended, as if to embrace it.

Picture 2: (CA=4.6 years; AE=8.3 years). In this picture, Anne demonstrates how quickly her abilities have developed. At the age of 4 years 6 months, her drawing is typical of the drawings of a child 8 years 3 months of age. She is clearly an alert, intelligent child. The person is fully drawn; Anne includes a head with stylized hair, a face with eyebrows, nose, mouth and neck. She places a smile on the face. The girl is clothed, a dress with a belt – illustrating an awareness of details in her social environment. The flower is an embellishment and suggests she has an active fantasy life. The neck indicates some self-awareness and regulation of her feelings. These are all signs of positive feelings about herself as a girl. All-in-all, Anne seems a happy child.

PICTURE 6   JENI, AGE 4-6

Picture 3. (CA = 4 years 10 months; AE = 5 years, 10 months). What has happened? Four months later, Anne draws an awful picture. It is a distorted, frightening and frightened figure. The picture is of a man – the head and body are disconnected---with a piggish nose, a mustache and a mouth full of teeth. The doubled eyes show terror. To a psychologist, this picture fits the criteria that imply Anne has had a traumatic sexual experience. The fragmentation of the head and facial features suggest dissociation, a "falling apart"; and, the funny, "piggish" nose suggests sexual displacement. The body is intact and calls attention to the phallic area. This is a drawing of an aggressive man with buttons down to the phallic area and with sharp, outreached, menacing fingers. This image suggests Anne is terrified and most likely having nightmares with images like this.

PICTURE 3: CA = 4.10 YEARS; AE = 5-10 YEARS

Picture 4 (CA = 5-0 year; AE = below age 5 years). Gone is the pretty, secure, happy girl. Strong dissociative feelings now dominate her sense of self and reactions to the environment. She is confused and concentration is difficult: the lines in the drawing are weak sketches, the body image is incomplete. The dissociation and splitting of her psyche into parts is depicted in the six figures, all floating about in the air. Note that the arms are cut off and the feet are weak, not connected. She has lost feelings of security and any sense that she controls or affects what happens what happens to her. Fantasy, memories and terror have invaded her consciousness.

Picture 4: CA = 5-0 Years: AE – Below 5 Years

Picture 5: (CA=5-1, CA = not score-able). Picture 5 shows a lasting terror, which remains four months after the trauma occurred. She remembers it vividly and is still overwhelmed by her experience. She no longer draws pictures of a pretty, secure and happy girl; instead this picture shows the head and neck of a frightened girl. The eyes are "seeing" but are fear-loaded and crying. The nose she draws is large, penile-shaped; it shows a displacement of the sexual trauma to the face; and, the mouth is full of teeth. It is an angry hurtful picture. The overemphasis on the neck indicates she is trying to distance her feelings from consciousness. She is trying to forget – to "cut-off" her feelings from bodily sensations.

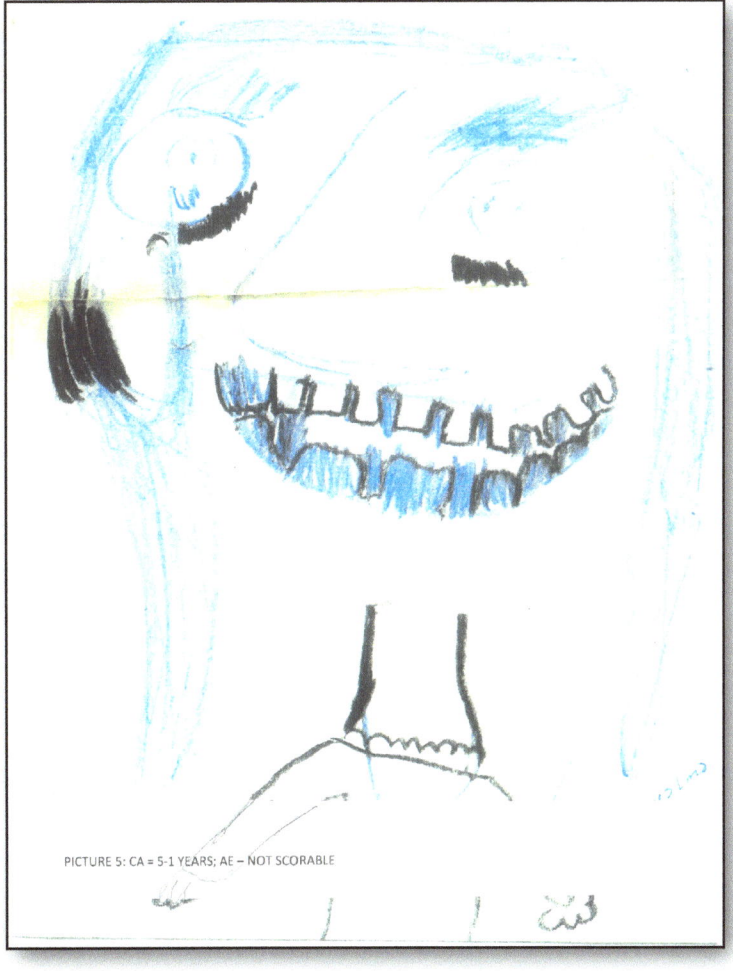

PICTURE 5: CA = 5-1 YEARS; AE – NOT SCORABLE

Picture 6: (CA=5-2; AE = 5.3 Years). What a picture! Anne makes a tremendous effort to externalize the traumatic event. She is telling her story. Actually, she is trying to tell her mother what happened, depicting all the details of a nude man in a bathroom, including toilet, bathtub, curtains on the window and a towel rack. Whatever happened may well have happened in a bathroom. She draws a naked man in full detail with breasts, underarm hair, belly button and genitals. There is a line from the genital area to the toilet. His hands are huge and awkward. A defensive displacement is taking place; there is a symbolic transfer to a penile-shaped nose. The neck is demarcated strongly, illustrating repression of feelings. She is trying emotionally to manage the trauma, to externalize the trauma, to be free of it, -- horrid as it must have been. It is a picture addressed to Mom, a call for help. The picture tells her story.

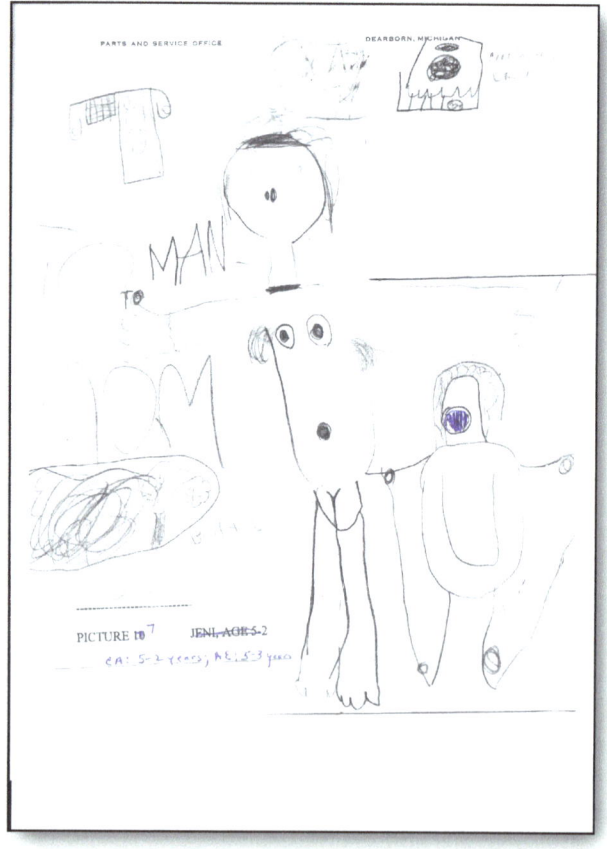

Picture 7: (CA=5-3: AE = approximately 6-7 Years) At least six months have passed since Anne had her secure world upset. No longer can she expect to feel safe, to trust her world is secure. She has had an experience that was too much for her conscious mind to accept; yet she must. As she adapts to this new, unsafe world, she tries to forget the actual event; the feelings remain because the psyche stores memories in symbolic form to calm the fears; now everyday experiences crowd into consciousness.

Anne now draws a girl. There are several clear signs of sexual trauma in this picture.[ix] The nose is unusually large with a "hole" on the end. This is an unusual drawing and signifies sexual awareness; and, the exaggerated, reddened and tightly closed mouth show damage there. The eyes are emphasized, closed or "hurting", a fear of seeing – or perhaps showing that what she sees hurts, scars the eyes. The neck that Anne draws is a strong indication of trying to cutoff bodily feelings, in an effort to forget what happened, and the large head is an attempt to rely on thinking. A new defense is taking hold as she works to squelch the memories, shown by the tight, orderly and compulsive markings on the arms, still outstretched, but without hands. In Anne's case, compulsiveness is an attempt to do everything just right, to squelch deeper, out-of-control feelings.

Have you noticed the lack of ears on all her pictures? So attentive to details, yet she does not show signs of hearing? I think this suggests an independent attitude that her parents noted early in her life – she does not want to be told what to do, she wants things her own way; and even in adulthood she has difficulty with authority – she likes to be independent in her work and world.

Picture 7: CA = 5.3 Years; AE = approximately 6.7 Years.

Picture 8. Anne seems to be feeling a somewhat better now. She does not draw the pretty picture that she drew when she was only four years old, but a smile returns to her face. Yet, evidence of the sexual trauma is still present – in symbolic form. She draws a penile-shaped nose with holes. The eyes are emphasized with red squares as if seeing hurts, she is trying to "box them" - to control what she sees. The closed, smiling mouth suggests a forced recovery of some pleasant feelings, to smile in spite of it all. Her arms are "flying," as if she is open for help, -"Pick me up, please." The cloud over her head suggests heaviness of her feelings; a depression hanging over her head. The recovery of fantasy and thinking abilities are there with the stars and yet, there is still a lack of feet; no sense of security has been recovered.

Picture 8: (CA = 5.4 Years; AE = 8.2 Years) Anne

Picture 9: (CA = 6-0 Years: AE = 5-3 Years) Now, over a year after the traumatic episode, Anne draws a complete lady in high heels and a big hat. It is a person too old for Anne's age. It is not a girl! Somewhere within her, she feels too old for her age – she knows too much for her age. She has regained some stability, her feet are grounded, and the stance is heavy planted. Her arms and hands show a clumsy recovery of strength. Yet the phallic nose remains, and the heavy black hat weighs on her head (depression). The signs of sexual trauma remain, cf., the phallic nose and clenched mouth.

The clothing decorations show that strong compulsive defenses have developed. The lines and color on the clothing depict increased compulsiveness – she is more determined to be right, to be in control. An overhanging depressive sense stays with her.

Picture 10: (CA = 6.3 Years; AE = over 11 Years) Picture 10 was selected from several drawn because it shows she has recovered a sense of "girlhood." The horror is not guarded against by forgetting and emotional defenses which now have become personality characteristics. The defenses include repression (forgetting) shown by the closed-off body at the neck, depression ("the heavy hat over the head"), compulsiveness (the over-patterned skirt) and a rigidity (the body stance). Signs of the sexual trauma remain – notice the pig-like nose and closed mouth.

Picture 9: CA=6.0 Years; AE = 5.3 Years

PICTURE 10: CA = 6-3 YEARS; AE = OVER 11 YEARS

Picture 10: CA = 6.3 Years; AE = over 11 Years

Picture 11: (CA = 8 Years; AE over 11 years). At eight years of age her defenses have become firm. She feels herself a small, insignificant girl within an overpowering environment. Going to the movies is fun, but notice a big heavy hat on a little head and a tightly closed mouth. The flowers are a good sign, suggesting that she can again indulge in fantasy, but obsessive and compulsive defenses remain strong. The picture had to be shortened because the original picture had 18 stories of the building and 134 windows – which she drew and counted.

PICTURE 11: CA = 8-0 YEARS; AE = OVER 11 YEARS

To summarize: These pictures identify that Anne was a precocious child who, at about 4 years 10 months of age, experienced a trauma. That the trauma was a sexual shock is verified in her drawings. Her recovery was a path from horror and nightmares to dissociation, and a tightening up of her emotional freedom and expressiveness. She lost a carefree spirit and innocence of childhood; her intelligence was temporarily blocked; the pleasant make-belief games of a child disappeared; and, fantasy life was dangerous for it brought horrid memories. She grew up too fast, her bodily sensations and feelings maturing before her spirit. It seemed opportune to discover how this event affected her adolescence and adulthood. We turn now to an interview with Anne when she was 45 years old.

An Interview with Anne at age 45

I had the occasion to interview Anne when she was 45 years old. I wanted perspective on the impact of the childhood trauma during her adolescent and adult years. She was a tall, attractive and poised lady – serious in demeanor. Anne seemed eager to share an overview of her life. She was living with her husband of 12 years; they had no children. She worked professionally in a managerial position. The following comments are culled from the interview:

According to Anne, her childhood years seemed unremarkable. She described herself as a quiet child in contrast to her younger, more energetic sister. School was easy and she was a good student; yet she did not like to study and would complete homework quickly. Anne vividly recalled times of feeling sad as a child, when she would be crying alone and wishing for consolation from her mother. She remembered no consolation, only aloneness. With a smile, she also recalled not wanting to be told what to do. She even tried to do chores before asked so that she would not be reminded. She still does not like someone else in authority. About six years of age, she told her older sister, "You don't have to tell me what to do. I am six years old." She needed control and resisted control by others.

Anne reported that her adolescence was socially difficult, partly because the family moved during her high school years. While she had a circle of friends, she did not often date; this was in contrast to her younger sister who always seemed to have a boyfriend. Anne described herself as "quietly rebellious" breaking parental boundaries, acting out, and indulging in both alcohol and marijuana use.

During later adolescence and college years Anne dated and sought some sexual activity. She described a few sexual encounters, none of them really satisfactory, with the exception of one encounter with a married professor. She remembers that she "passed out" during intercourse. She had no memory of the feelings, just a sense of wonder. Otherwise she reported no climactic response. Her first attempt at a sexual relationship lasted only a couple months. She reported that the love-making was somewhat abusive.

Anne reported that she was attracted to immigrants, and that they "turned her on." Her first marriage was to a Turkish man whom she described as "a handsome, dark-haired man. She enjoyed intercourse with him, but she was physically unresponsive. The marriage lasted about four years. They divorced. Then, in one sexual encounter between marriages, she again "passed out" during intercourse, but again had no memory of the feelings, not even immediately afterwards. About eight years later, she married a French immigrant and this marriage has lasted. Professionally she has been quite successful, although changing professional positions several times during her adult years.

Her second marriage worked better. He, too, was an immigrant - we can only wonder at her attraction to "aliens." It seems an attraction to strangeness, or rather to the strangeness of her first experience with sexual feelings when she was traumatized. This partner took time to make love and gradually brought sexual feelings to the fore. She remembers vividly her first experienced climax – it was so gratifying, she jumped out of bed – amazed and elated.

Anne has had therapy over a period of several years during her adulthood. During her therapy a memory of being in a bathroom with a "big, dark man" and being scared, emerged; this seems the origin of her trauma. It was a relative whom she rarely saw, thankfully; he was known as a person who liked children. Now, in her forties, she agreed to draw several pictures of a person for this study.

She drew two pictures during the interview. Her artistic talent remains obvious in these two pictures. The pictures have excellent proportion with lines finely drawn, tenuous and overworked. Picture 12 presents a poised, business-woman with stylish dress and a large hat. The person is facing forward, meeting the world in a direct manner. Yet, the sketchy, tenuous lines are either the result of artistic technique and/or represent tenuousness and insecurity in her self-concept as she faces the world. The person seems rigid, with the hat still there, suggesting that a depressive core remains. Subtle signs of sexual trauma remain. For instance, the two dots in the nose are still there! Scars of trauma lessen yet do not disappear, not even over a lifetime.

Picture12: CA = 45 Years   Picture 13: CA = 45 Years

The second picture is quite in contrast to the first. Here she presents a woman dancing, graceful, almost floating and without constraints. There seems to be "two sides" to Anne, a split between the controlled, professional person and the freer, wished-to-be person. Internally, she holds onto a sense of a carefree freedom fantasized in childhood. Even here, on this picture, the emphasis on the nose remains. Hands are missing, suggesting she has not found a means of satisfying her internal fantasies and expectations. The schism between the reality-oriented business-person and the free-spirited fantasy dancer may even yet cause anxieties and unsatisfied fantasies.

Summary of analysis of drawings

The age-equivalent scores on the DAP (Draw-a-Picture) Test indicate that up to the age of 4 ½ years, she was far ahead of other children in drawing abilities. Her intelligence seemed in the superior range. Then, within four months her scores dropped to average, demonstrating a significant blocking of her intellectual abilities, probably of learning as well. It took about a year before her scores again reflected superior intellect and before her cognitive skills recovered.

The qualitative analysis of the pictures demonstrated the intrusion of a trauma into her emotional life, thought processes, and coincidentally her drawing ability. The horror depicted in Pictures 4, 5 and 6 demonstrate the effect of a trauma. Being overwhelmed by fright must have interfered with her everyday behavior, but the parents seemed unaware of the experience. A conjecture about her behavior as a child during this period would support a period of withdrawal and/or clinginess to her parents for there is little aggressive behavior in the drawings. She became careful and cautious, represented by compulsive traits that developed – a sign of the desire for greater control over her feelings and actions.

There is no doubt that she experienced a sexual trauma. The significant indices are present: the elongated nose, the pig-like nose, distortions and/or emphasis of the mouth, and, unusual, unfinished, incomplete drawings of the body.

Three

Discussion of the Effects of the Trauma

To return to our story. Anne was sexually traumatized at an early age. Lost in her memory were details of the exact event which emerged to pattern her behavior throughout her life. So intense was her reaction, she experienced a breakdown of her personality – as shown in her drawings that depicted a temporary dissociative state.[x] Gratefully, Anne did not continue to be abused, although many children are.

The psychological effects of the traumatic experience on Anne are clear: horror was followed by dissociation. Fears of oral aggression emerged, as indicated by sharp teeth. With the dissociation, repression became necessary and is evident in Picture 6 as she tried to "cut-off" feelings. Then, there was an attempt to externalize the event (Picture 7), to tell the story. At the same time, attempts to forget brought repression that in turn provided an emotional means to manage the experience. The result was a rigidity and compulsiveness manifested in her drawings as means of controlling unwanted memories. A strong need for control developed – both to contain her feelings and to exert order to her external world.

Her development resumed when she was able to externalize the event through her drawings, and then to contain the fright through the development of defense mechanisms, as the compulsiveness and need to control circumstances.

One unexpected effect of the traumatic episode is a time rhythm that was instilled in her life. The unconscious event patterned her behavior throughout life to become anxious about every four to five years, affecting her present life. This patterning has been called an "anniversary reaction." The actual event remains unconscious in cases but the emotional impact comes through. For instance, Anne's trauma came when she was four to five years old; she has had difficulty remaining in a personal relationship or professional employment more than four to five years. Her first marriage was terminated after four years. Her second marriage was severely discordant after four to five years, and nine-to-ten years. Her employment pattern also showed changes and/or difficulties following a similar timeline. These were anniversary reactions of the trauma. It is to her credit, and superior intelligence, that her commitment to therapy helped sustain her marriage, her professional life and her sense of self.

Physical difficulties are common for those who experience traumatic events. Anne developed a thyroid problem and skin ailments that proved chronic. In this case, the chronic ailments may well have some origin in the repression of affect following the trauma.

Four

RECOVERY

Anne apparently recovered well from her traumatic event. She is a productive member of society, enjoys a stable, secure relationship with her partner, and has a successful professional position. There were many steps through which she passed on the path to renewing positive feelings about herself. Anne has been very fortunate. Her family is a tightly-knit family which has supported each other through many a misstep and also for the accomplishment of each. In addition, she continues in therapy, working to understand and smoothen the pathways of adulthood. Her relationships with men have provided the greatest anxieties and problems as she has worked incessantly to undo the lasting damage of the original trauma. She was eager to share her story.

The following steps are recommended throughout the literature on dealing with trauma.

Finding a Safe Place:

The child, or adult, first flees for safety. The flight may be to a parent or other adult or to a safe place – in a closet, under the bed, just somewhere away from the place of trauma. Finding safety, is a search for security, and then for comfort. Even for a child who has been threatened not to tell, he/she may seek the physical comfort from a trusted parent – and not tell what has frightened them. The comforting, accepting love of a trusted, warm adult can calm the fears and terror. In Anne's case, safety was found with her parents who, without being aware of the event, would have sensed her distress and comforted her.

Facing the Fears:

To let one's self know and re-feel the horror of a trauma is to have the courage to acknowledge the helplessness that strikes. To acknowledge what happened, to accept the horror, is the first step in recovery. As a rabbit may "freeze" when chased by a fox, and thus be caught, a person may freeze when the trauma has no escape. To freeze is to become "robot-like." It is an inability to move, to change the situation. Actions and feelings are frozen. This effect as related to trauma has been suggested by Porges (2011): the neurological system has an *immobilization defense system*, that is, the fight-flight response system to stress has a "freeze" component. This automatic response to trauma, when fight and flight are unavailable, may result in a "freezing", - an immobilization of the nervous pathways related to stress. Without significant help at the time of trauma, the effects may become permanent – in that similar stimuli may trigger the same reaction that followed the event – emotionally and cognitively as well as physiologically. For a child, "frozen fears" are not unusual because they have fewer, less powerful strength for escape.

Telling the story:

A first step in recovery is the opportunity for and ability of the child to talk to someone what happened. Ideally, the person would be a parent(s) from whom the child has previously received support, comfort, tenderness, and care. The person must be able to listen, to encourage the child to talk about the event – and without the impulse to deny or disbelieve the child. The listener will accept the child's expression of feelings; try to avoid soothing before the story is completed; and, reflect back to the child, the child's emotional reactions.

Acceptance leads to soothing, to calming the child's fears and can then be followed by a plan of action that relieves the child's fears and anxiety.

There are many ways to tell the story. Creative expression of the event provide emotional release for the overwrought feelings. Drawings, dancing, music, words open the gates of horror and may release the emotional and thought-loaded tensions. Expression, serves to lessen the hold of the trauma on the person. Denial that it happened gives the terror more inward control.

Resilience:

Resilience refers to the mental, emotional and behavioral ability to adapt to stressful events. Anne showed a remarkable resilience, considering the degree of interference with her psychological functioning. With regard to the presence of resilience in childhood, Wolff (1995) states:

> Resilience is an enduring aspect of the person. Genetic and other constitutionally based qualities both determine and are in turn modified by life experiences. Good intelligence plays a major part in developing resilience as does an easy, adaptable sociable temperament that, together with an appealing appearance, attract positive responses from others which in turn contribute to that inner sense of self-worth, competence and self-efficacy that has repeatedly been identified as a vital component of resilience. The sources of such positive responses are threefold: primary relationships within the family; the network of relationships with adults and children outside the family; and competence and achievement. (p.56)
>
> Anne manifest much resilience in her turning to everyday activities. Family and school provided guidance for her behavior. Changing expectations and circumstances were welcome relief for her.

Intelligence:

A review of research by Condly (2008) reinforces that intelligence and a prior easy temperament are primary factors for resilience. As the precocious child that she proved herself to be, (cf. her drawings) she passed through crisis and turned her attention to achievement in school.

Supportive Environment:

The degree of support given by parents, family, and social environment is important. With the family, the support can be open; it is clearly recognized that a previously secure attachment is important for working through traumata. Anne's parents were present for her, even though unaware of the event. A positive, predictable social environment, such as the school, also may be a place of comfort, free from stimuli that may provoke recall of the traumatic incident.

Prior personality strengths:

Anne's ego development was firm prior to the incident. She seemed a happy, self-confident child. While the sexual trauma she experienced was not continuous or severe in terms of physical damage, the emotional reaction was severe and permanent. And the fact that her parents provided emotional and physical security were undoubtedly helpful for her recovery. As reported by Condly (2008), high intelligence is not a perfect protective factor against trauma. He reports that: "Resilient children of high intelligence…seem to suffer more emotional distress and depression" (p.216). He also states that highly intelligent children are more sensitive to environmental situations and may suffer greater symptoms of internal stress, leaving the child more vulnerable to emotional scarring and the internalization of stress. It is true that throughout Anne's life, both in her personal and professional life, she has struggled to remain the happy, secure person with which she began life.

Psychotherapy:

The depression that Anne experienced after the event has followed her throughout her adulthood, even though it has significantly lessened over the years, due in part to her intense therapeutic efforts. For the child, to confront these emotionally charged, damaging events, it is often desirable, even necessary, to seek professional help. The need to recover and express the event, to place it in perspective to one's life, and to regain self-confidence is often a primary recuperative process.

Physiological reaction:

The research that covers the physiological results of sexual trauma during childhood indicates that signs of these events may remain present throughout the life of the person. While the frequency, severity, and relationship with the child are important for identifying the life-long effects, and even with less severe traumata, there are often disturbing residues of the trauma. In Anne's case, the chronic difficulties with her thyroid function may well have some origin in the suppression of affect following the sexual trauma. Further, she developed psoriasis after becoming sexually active in her teenage years – a reaction that she experiences as a self-protective mechanism against further trauma.

Remaining Effects:

For Anne, the schism that remains in her perception of herself includes a split between pragmatic ego functioning and a superego ideal. The highly functioning business persona is at odds with her fantasized ideal, which seems a re-vitalizing of childhood freedom and innocence. Over the years, the conscious reinforcement of an unrealistic sense of possible escape has resulted in patterns of tension, anxieties, and life dissatisfaction that build up over a period of 4-5 years.

Five

THE PSYCHOLOGICAL EFFECTS OF ANY TRAUMA

A trauma of any kind changes a personality – at any age. Return to the prior level of functioning is not often possible, for the psyche has been damaged. The scars that remain skew the personality, although a return to an apparent well-functioning person may come. Trauma is an insult to the psychophysiological system. Envision the tripartite psyche as a circle with the basic parts at the core (id), surrounded by the ego with its reality view, and the outer part as the conscience or superego with the emphasis on social expectations. Trauma slices through the superego –conscience is damaged - social expectations are destroyed. Good and bad become confused. Wariness develops, and even paranoid tendencies can arise.

Trauma then changes the ego - the view of the world is changed. With this, comes an awareness that the world, one's reality, is not predictable, may even be dangerous. The real world now includes the possibility of unexpected damaging or hurtful experiences or bad people – especially in similar situations as the trauma. Security disappears; innocence is gone. Any similar situation may evoke memories and feelings of the traumatic event.

The damage to the view of reality loosens the ego defenses that held once unwelcome impulses at bay. Without the socially appropriate defenses, the restriction against "acting out" of impulsive feelings against the self or others is tempered, even lost. To act out impulses is no longer forbidden for impulses have been acted out against the person. Whether it be aggression, lies, distrust nothing seems "bad" for bad was done to the person. Psychic functioning is damaged, leaving scars. The degree of psychic damage is usually relative to prior personality characteristics, and the severity of the trauma (how much of the psychic whole is damaged), and the balm for healing that follows.

A final note: One misconception that is generally held is that the traumatized person can "get over" it. It is commonly held that people can get over of the trauma, forget it ever happened, and go on with their lives as if it never happened, as "just get over of It". Soldiers back from the war are told, "It's over. You are back home." "It won't happen here." "You are safe. "But the reality is, it is not over. It lives *within* and *with* the traumatized person. The trauma must be integrated into the personality, not to be disbelieved or the importance denied by others. The trauma will be integrated into the person's life, not *extracted* from memory. When the memories are denied, the trauma deepens its hold on the person. It takes charge of the person in undesirable, unknown ways.

Some children regain a sense of security and sense of self after abuse, sometimes even after severe abuse. Most are not as fortunate and struggle throughout life, yearning for inner contentment and longing for love to heal the bruises.

To end on a positive note, Anne and many other children, can resume a normal path of development, provided the pathway for recovery. To date, Anne is a happier, freer person and more self-directed than ever before. Her creativity has resumed, her professional life is more satisfactory and her relationships more enjoyable.

Footnotes

i   "Child Maltreatment 2012," U.S. Department of Health and Human Services. Administration for Children and Families, Administration on Children. Youth and Families, Children's Bureau.

ii   "When a Child Tells about Sexual Abuse: What Protective Adults need to Know" (2014). http://www.stopitnow.org/whenachildtells.

iii   Official California Legislative Information, California Law, California Penal Code, Section 281-289.6, heep://www.leginfo.ca.gov/dgi-bin/disp laycode?section=pen&group-00001

iv   Refer to "The Neurological Legacy of Childhood Trauma" by Maggie Brown in PLOS/Blogs at http://blogs.plos.org/speakingof medicine/2012/06/01/ the-neurological-legacy-of-childhood...

v   For an in-depth discussion of trauma, see Freud, S. (1917) "Fixation upon traumas: the unconscious." In *Introductory Lectures on Psychoanalysis, Lecture CVIII.* Standard Edition, 16, 273-285a, p. 252

vi   See Jack A. Naglieri (1988) *Draw a Person: A Quantitative Scoring System.* San Antonio, Texas: Psychological Corporation. Please note that while the norms are well established, the interpretation of any drawing is complex and requires extensive psychological training and experience.

vii   I first became aware of the scoring system for sexual trauma in children from Dr. Mary Sue Moore who used the system developed by Dr. Brendan McCarthy of the Tavistock Centre in London, England and was provided to me by Dr. Mary Sue Moore of Boulder, Colorado. These scoring procedures are found in Naglieri, Jack A., McNeish, T.J. & Bardon, and A.V.

(1991) *Draw A Person: Screening Procedure for Emotional Disturbance.* San Antonio Texas: Psychological Corporation.

vii "Sufferers of this rare condition (dissociation) are usually victims of severe abuse." Refer to::
https://www.psychologytoday.com/conditions2014.

References

Burt, C. (1921) *Mental and Scholastic Tests*. London: P.S.King & Son as quoted in *Silent Screams and Hidden Cries* by Agnes Wohl and Bobbie Kaufman. 1985. Brunner/Mazel, Inc., New York.

Condly, Steven J. (2008) "Resilience in Children. A Review of Literature with Implications for Education" (2006) in *Urban Education, 41, 211-236*.

Goodenough, F. (1926) *Measurement of intelligence by drawings*. New York: Harcourt, Brace and World.

Koppitz, E. (1968) *Psychological evaluation of children's drawings*. New York: Grune & Stratton.

Naglieri, Jack A. (1998) *Draw A Person: A quantitative scoring system*. San Antonio, Texas; Psychological Corporation.

Naglieri, Jack A., McNeish, T.J., & Bardon, A.V. (1991) *Draw A Person: Screening Procedure for Emotional Disturbance*. San Antonio, Texas: Psychological Corporation.

Porges, Stephen W. "The Polyvagal Perspective" in *Biol Psychol* 2007 Feb. 74(2):116-143

Wolff, S. (1995) "The Concept of Resilience" Australian and New Zealand Journal of Psychiatry. 29(4) pp. 565-574

About the Author

Viola Mecke, PhD, ABPP is a clinical psychologist with over forty years' experience in teaching and in clinical practice. She was a Clinical Professor Emerita (adjunct) in the Department of Psychiatry and Behavioral Sciences at Stanford University Medical School and Emerita Professor of Educational Psychology at the East Bay California State University. She is currently retired from clinical practice and devotes her time to consultation and writing. She has two previous books published: *Fatal Attachments: The Instigation to Suicide*, published by Praeger Publishers *in 2004* and *Aging Wisely: Facing Emotional Challenges from 50 to 85+ Years*, published by XLibris LLC, in 2013.

Her field of specialty has focused on emotional and personality development throughout the life span. Working with children and in psychotherapy with families has been a center of her work. While working in therapy with children, she became aware of the complexity of the child's reactions to incidents in their lives and to family interactions.

One special concern has been to understand the effects of trauma and illness upon children, and the subsequent effects on their development. A child's drawings often reflect, through symbolic representation, their inner concerns and anxieties – symbolic because fear hides the actual memory. This is a story of one young girl, a precocious child who apparently had one significant, overpowering event that colored her understanding of people and patterns of behavior throughout her life.

Dr. Mecke is presently retired and lives in Santa Barbara.

She can be contacted through email: EVB1@cox.net

Appendix

Additional Pictures

There were over 200 pictures that Anne had drawn. Here are a few more example that illustrate her distress.

CA = 5 years 6 months. A woman with a bee on her nose!

CA = 5 years, 9 months

CA = five years, 11 months

www.ingramcontent.com/pod-product-compliance
Lightning Source LLC
Chambersburg PA
CBHW050753290526
45792CB00008B/2160

* 9 7 8 1 5 1 5 3 3 1 2 6 1 *